New Consensus for Old

New Consensus for Old
Cultural Studies from Left to Right

Thomas Frank

PRICKLY PARADIGM PRESS
CHICAGO

An earlier version of this pamphlet was published as chapter
eight of *One Market Under God* (Doubleday, 2000).

Prickly Paradigm Press, LLC
5629 South University Avenue
Chicago, Il 60637

www.prickly-paradigm.com

ISBN: 0-9717575-4-2
LCCN: 2002 102651

Printed in the United States of America on acid-free
paper.

George was touched by the Fair. He stood one night with Charles Nolan, watching the crowds of the Midway, and dreamed aloud: the people had done all this! It was "of the people, by the people, for the people!" The lawyer argued: "No, most of the money was subscribed by rich men. The people had nothing to do with designing the buildings." The economist pulled his beard and sighed. Anyhow, the people were enjoying it....Perhaps the Kingdom of God was a little nearer.

—Henry George's visit to the 1894 Columbian Exposition, according to Thomas Beer, *The Mauve Decade* (1926)

The sociologist Herbert Gans had been writing about popular culture and its audiences for some twenty years when he published his 1974 book *Popular Culture and High Culture*, a 159-page summary of his thinking on the subject. The volume is now twenty-eight years old, and it builds on arguments Gans had been making since the '50s, but if not for a number of bad calls and an obsolete jargon it could have been written yesterday, so reliably does it predict certain dominant scholarly concerns of our own times. For Gans, as for so many academic writers about culture, the longstanding American debate over high culture and mass culture was really a broader clash between elitism and populism, between the snobbish tastes of the educated and the functional democracy of popular culture. Gans began the book by rejecting the idea "that popular culture is simply imposed on the audience from above," that a malign culture industry is able to tell us what to think. In fact, he argues, audiences have the power to demand and receive, through the medium of the market, the culture of their choosing from the entertainment industry. Then, in what would eventually become the trademark gesture of academic cultural studies, Gans hammered the *critics* of the entertainment industry as the real villains, as "elitist" nabobs who are "unhappy with [recent] tendencies toward cultural democracy" and who obnoxiously assume they know what is best for the world. The real subject of cultural debate is thus the attitude of the critic, in particular his or her faith in the intelligence of the audience. And for holding audiences in inexcusably low esteem Gans scolded mid-century critic Dwight

Macdonald and Herbert Marcuse, late of the famous "Frankfurt School" of Marxist social theory.

Up to this point Gans seems to have anticipated with uncanny accuracy the issues, the preconceptions, and even the villains of academic cultural criticism of the '90s. But his streak of prescience ends when he predicts that the elitist mass culture critique he identifies with Macdonald and Marcuse would stage a triumphant return in the very near future. Gans arrived at this prediction by connecting the mass culture critique, as a theory that celebrates the transcendent worth of a canonical education and good taste, with the interests of intellectuals generally: when their "status" is under attack or in decline, they revert naturally to the old elitism, dreaming up all sorts of highbrow bushwa about art and culture in order to reinforce the hierarchies that support their exalted social position. But when respect for intellectuals is on the rise, they can lighten up, make peace with middle America, and read *USA Today* along with the rest of us.

In fact this is almost exactly the opposite of what actually happened in the '90s, when the "culture wars" brought the humanities under the fiercest attack they had endured in generations. Yes, academic professionalism did indeed seem to grow more and more pronounced with each assault from the family-values right. Think of the clotted, ciphered academic prose style—a reliable source of amusement for journalists throughout the decade—that knotted itself ever more egregiously with each blustering new chapter of the culture wars. The object of all this credential-flashing, sentence-mangling expertise, however, was not the sanctity of high culture, but precisely the opposite. Academics of the '90s loved popular culture. They did not sneer. Rather, they declared their fandom in the most earnest of tones and most sophisticated of theoretical formulations. Popular culture was not only democratic, they believed, it was downright counter-hegemonic. Meanwhile the mass culture critique that Gans so abhorred did not reappear in the '90s; on the contrary, scholars joined journalists, politicians, and media moguls in pounding it relentlessly, in dispatching it off to that special oblivion reserved for intellectual anathema.

Rumble with the Cult Studs

Let's start with *Highbrow/Lowbrow*, the influential 1988 book in which historian Lawrence Levine argued that the problem of aesthetic elitism was in fact the central drama of American cultural history. By parading before readers a series of vignettes in which repulsive, upper-class nineteenth-century snobs—each of them coupled carefully with his racist and otherwise offensive remarks—looked to high culture for a refuge from democracy, Levine sought to prove that hierarchies of taste were analogous to social hierarchy generally and to racism specifically. What the high culture patrons of the past set out to do was to make audiences "less interactive," to transform them from "a public" into "a group of mute receptors." Historian Andrew Ross carried both the argument and the rhetorical strategy into the twentieth century in his 1989 book *No Respect*, continuing to find in virtually any iteration of highbrow taste a tacit expression of contempt for democracy.

As the '90s unfolded, it soon became clear that the signature scholarly gesture of our time was not some warmed over aestheticism, but a populist celebration of the power and "agency" of audiences and fans, of their ability to evade the grasp of the makers of mass culture, and of their talent for transforming just about any bit of cultural detritus into an implement of rebellion. Although cultural populism appeared everywhere in academia, its best known and loudest proponents were the various celebrities of the rapidly growing discipline known as cultural studies—the "cult studs," to use the phrase of one canny reviewer. Like Gans, the cult studs tended to be unremittingly hostile to the elitism and hierarchy that older ways of understanding popular culture seemed to imply; they tended to see audience "agency" lurking in every consumer decision. They were able to find seeds of rebellion and resistance in almost any of the culture-products once scoffed at as "lowbrow," and accordingly they turned their attention from the narrow canon of "highbrow" texts to the vast prairies of popular culture. British academic Jim McGuigan has described this central article of the cult-stud's faith as a formulaic "populist reflex," a tendency to judge any thought, proposal, or text by this overarching standard: What does this imply about the power of the people? Accounts of popular culture in which shoppers twit shopkeepers, say, or sitcom viewers think subversive thoughts, or fans of boy bands grow suspicious of patriarchy are to be celebrated and affirmed for their democratic implications. On the other hand, accounts of popular culture in which audiences are tricked, manipulated, or otherwise made to act against their best interests are automatically "'elitist,'" as the distinguished cult stud Lawrence Grossberg once put it (in a line echoed in almost every cultural studies essay or book I have ever read), because they assume that audiences are "necessarily silent, passive, political and cultural dopes."

Generally speaking, cult studs do not frequently apply the term "elitist" to Hollywood executives or TV producers. This is a characteristic they attribute not to the culture industries but to *critics* of the

culture industries, most notably the same gang of
easy-to-hate Frankfurt School Marxists that so pissed
off Herbert Gans back in 1974. Cult studs tend to
see in the work of Marcuse and fellow Frankfurter
Theodor Adorno (who once, to his undying infamy,
denounced jazz) the very embodiment of the snobbery from which academia was only now recovering.
In reaction to the uptight squareness of the
Frankfurters, the cult-stud community wasted no
opportunity to marvel at the myriad sites of "resistance" found in TV talk shows, sci-fi fandom, rock
videos, fashion magazines, shopping malls, comic
books, and the like, describing the most innocent-
looking forms of entertainment as hotly contested
battlegrounds of social conflict. Their books teem
with stories of aesthetic hierarchies rudely over-
turned; with subversive mallwalkers dauntlessly using
up the mall's air conditioning; with heroic fans
building their workers' paradise right there in the
Star Trek corpus; with rebellious readers of women's
fashion magazines symbolically smashing the state.
As Michael Bérubé summarized the discipline's focus
in 1992:

> It is always attempting...to discover and interpret the
> ways disparate disciplinary subjects *talk back*: how
> consumers deform and transform the products they

use to construct their lives; how "natives" rewrite and trouble the ethnographies of (and *to*) which they are subject....

For all their populism, though, the cult studs tend to be remarkably professional-minded. In fact, they are perhaps the least public group of intellectuals ever to come down the pike. This is something that goes far beyond an excessive use of difficult academic jargon. Cult studs may be nominally interested in the films of King Vidor or risqué comic books, but by far the most attractive subject to them (judging by the number of pages and books given over to it) is cultural studies itself: where it came from, what its proper subject is, whether it even exists or not. Actual cultural interpretation invariably takes a back seat to long-winded theoretical maneuverings. A good example is *We Gotta Get Out of This Place*, a 1992 book by Grossberg that is ostensibly about rock 'n' roll, but that begins by plodding through a remarkable 127 pages of theoretical hedging— paying homage to all the right texts; identifying and avoiding the errors of this school and that; situating itself with relationship to Foucault, Gramsci, Deleuze and Guattari, and, yes, Kant—before taking up "the political possibilities of rock." Other cult-stud texts wonder endlessly about the nature of "disciplinarity" and the correct role of intellectuals in society, but seem always to come to the same conclusion. Namely, that boundaries between academic disciplines are false and reactionary, and that, since cult studs often write on subjects not traditionally under the purview of the (English) departments by which they are employed, there's something really revolutionary about them. So urgently do cult studs believe this point needs to be made that there are actually several books dedicated to it alone, each of which makes abundant use of the connected theme of cult stud as a figure persecuted for crossing disciplinary boundaries. One 1996 anthology, *Disciplinarity and Dissent*, begins with a mournful evocation of those who fell victim to the scourge of disciplinarity in previous decades, moves on to tell the arduous history of cultural studies, recounts the expertise, "training," and "disciplinary exile" of each of the volume's contributors, and then offers, in a curious move from persecution fantasy to oracular wisdom, this bit of credentialing advice:

> For someone interested in sociology and cultural studies...it would not be helpful to study sociology at the University of Illinois at Urbana-Champaign or at the University of Wisconsin, but it might well be helpful to study it at the University of California at Santa Barbara.

Critical knowledge indeed for a young person preparing to spend a lifetime on the front lines of popular resistance. It will be on the exam for sure.

The contradiction between the discipline's populism and its resolute institution-mindedness occasionally returns to bite the cult studs in the ass. It makes possible excruciating moments like the one recounted in 1995 by Richard Hoggart, one of the founders of the field, in which a "distinguished scholar from England" who was giving a paper at a cultural studies conference in America found himself "interrupted by a group of women graduate students who mounted the platform and demanded access to the microphone."

> They objected, they said, to any more "so-called experts" being allowed to speak from the rostrum when they had not been invited to do so. They demanded equal rights on the ground that their opinions were, as a matter of principle and fact, as good as anyone else's; to have only "established specialists" giving papers was "unacceptable academic elitism."

The core features of the cult-stud approach come into high relief when we contrast the discipline's foundational text, the 788-page *Cultural Studies*

anthology of 1992, with the slightly less gigantic
Mass Culture anthology of 1957, a standard assigned
text of an earlier era which also took on the then-
novel subject of popular culture. While the older
book was organized according to the different
industries covered (film, magazine publishing,
advertising, TV, etc.) and while it lumped together
essays originally published in popular magazines
along with contributions to the *American Journal of
Sociology*, the 1992 book is an impressively precise
record of just about everything uttered at an academic conference that took place one heroic week in
1990, organized alphabetically by the contributors'
names. Nearly all are academics. The central theme
of the later book is not so much "culture" as its
"study"; not the liveliness of "the Popular Arts" but
the shimmering genius of culture's interlocutors.
The tome's brick-like size and weight make its
message hard to miss: this is the cornerstone of a
grand new professional edifice, complete with a
language, purview, and theory that are uniquely its
own. These days the earlier, more popular book is
faulted for being an elitist showplace, a museum of
the mass culture critique (it includes scornful essays
by both Dwight Macdonald and Theodor Adorno).
But the later, infinitely more populist volume (one
of its more annoying themes is that the critic must

also be a fan) seems to have been constructed without any concern at all for the reading public. It was only revised, its editors note, so that the participants in the conference could clarify their statements, sharpen their positions.

But while the cult studs enshrined their brand of populism as the pedagogy of choice in the early '90s, hounding the mass culture critique from the field and establishing their notions of agency and resistance as interpretative common sense, neither Herbert Gans nor anyone else from the sociological school with which he is identified was invited to the victory party. Gans' 1974 book may have been a direct antecedent of the bumper crop of cult-stud monographs and anthologies that were issued in the '90s, but you will search those later books in vain for references to Gans and his colleagues. This is especially curious given the cult studs' compulsive reciting of influences and intellectual genealogy. Gans is not mentioned in either the vast bibliography or the index of the gigantic foundational anthology; he does not appear at all in Patrick Brantlinger's 1990 history of cultural studies, in Grossberg's 1992 account of the history of cultural studies, in Stanley Aronowitz's 1993 account of the history of cultural studies, in Simon During's 1993 anthology on the history of cultural studies, in John Fiske's 1993 book on cultural studies and history, in Angela McRobbie's 1994 account of the history of cultural studies, in Jeffrey Williams' 1995 anthology on the culture wars and cultural studies, or in Cary Nelson and Dilip Gaonkar's 1996 anthology on academia and the history of cultural studies.

Why are he and the other sociologists of the 1950s left out? Simple: because of the insufficient radicalism of Gans' generation. Cultural studies, as its proponents let you know with tiresome frequency, is a proudly committed leftist pedagogy; it is what cult-stud pooh-bah Simon During calls "an engaged discipline." Herbert Gans, meanwhile, hails from an academic tradition that (to simplify ruthlessly) imagined itself as just the opposite. The "consensus" scholars of his day tended not to boast of their own subversiveness, but to downplay social conflict in order to emphasize a vision of a healthy and well-functioning national whole. In books like Daniel Bell's *End of Ideology* and Richard Hofstadter's *Age of Reform* the consensus thinkers (no studs they) portrayed dissent as disease; in public places like *Partisan Review* they more or less abandoned their adolescent leftism and enlisted in the American Century.

Cult studs can imagine nothing more reprehensible. The very idea of consensus is intellectual poison in our time, attacked ferociously by management theorists like Tom Peters and mocked in TV advertising and Hollywood film alike. And in the works of the cult studs the consensus era comes off as a time of scholarly practice so degraded it is scarcely worth remembering. Cult stud Patrick Brantlinger, for example, recalls in *Crusoe's Footprints* how the discipline of American Studies (a slightly older rival of cultural studies) was founded in the years after World War II as a deliberate venture in national myth-making and rips it as "an academic cultural chauvinism" whose "ultimate goal," despicably, was "social harmony." Lawrence Levine runs over the same story again in his 1996 book on the culture wars, tarring American Studies as nothing less than premeditated intellectual collaboration with the Cold War state. Nelson and Gaonkar remember it as a "McCarthy-era pact [with "state power"] guaranteeing silence and irrelevance from the humanities and collaboration from the social sciences...." By contrast, any proper cult stud is out to develop, as Henry Giroux once put it, "a radical politics of difference," to revel in cultural and identity fragmentation, to pose boldly on the ramparts of the culture wars, to provoke and savor the denunciations of hysterical fundamentalists.

The cult studs may have lifted their populist approach whole cloth from the mild-mannered scholarship of the Eisenhower era, but given their transgressive, decentering mission, it is simply inconceivable that they should ever acknowledge Gans and his consensus crowd. No, they must have an intellectual lineage more in keeping with their status as the *ne plus ultra* in counter-hegemony, and so when the occasion arises (as it does very, very frequently) to track their pedigree, the cult studs nearly always find themselves to descend not from the plodding drayhorses of American sociology but from the purest-blooded barricade-charging European stallions.

Still, the ghost of consensus will not rest. We may hear of how the cult studs stand on the front lines of political confrontation; we may gape at the wounds inflicted by the reactionaries upon their noble corpus; but we cannot help noticing that the noise from the front sounds a lot like somebody shaking a big chunk of sheet metal just behind the curtain.

Then Came Empowerment

The cult studs may fancy themselves the fightin'est, shootin'est, transgressin'est bunch of hell-raisers since Mao himself, but when their trademark arguments about audience agency are considered in the context of the larger culture, their vanguardist boasting starts to seem a little hollow. Readers familiar with American business culture in particular must be impressed not with cultural studies' radicalism, but with its ordinariness, with how well cultural studies complimented the emerging

consensus of New Economy thought. If one's radicalism is to be measured by how much one upsets
the Christian right or diverges from the traditional
highbrow canon, then okay, maybe the cult studs
are in the running for the title. But if we look
beyond the angry pantomime of the culture wars,
what we find is a corporate right that itself had no
use for the traditional canons of good taste, that
gave nary a damn for family values, that *agreed* with
the cult studs on the revolutionary power of popular
culture and the nobility of subjects who "talked
back," that gloried in symbolic assaults on propriety,
on brokers, on bankers, on old-style suit-wearers of
all descriptions.

From the feverish business radicalism of *Fast
Company* to the homely faith of the Beardstown
Ladies, a populist reflex dominated the landscape of
'90s corporate thought as well as high academic
criticism. There, too, it was agreed that Americans
inhabited an age of radical democratic transforma-
tion, of multiculturalism and righteous subalterns;
that we could no longer tolerate top-down organi-
zational hierarchies; that no error outranked the
moral crime of elitism, defined there as the bureau-
crats' arrogant belief that they knew better than the
consumer, stockholder, or audience. There, too, the

language and imagery of production was being effaced by that of consumption; class by classism; democracy by interactivity. Listening executives were joining forces with "change agents" to see to it that we were all "empowered." And the right of audiences to "talk back" to the CEO (through stock-holding) or to the brand manager (through the focus group) was trumping all other economic rights and claims that publics might conceivably assert.

This market populism was unambiguously a discourse of the right. Its purpose was to grab democratic legitimacy for the business world, to downplay the age-old public suspicion of big business and instead to characterize whatever corporate management wanted to do as the will of the people. When it spoke of popular participation in stock markets, it did so in order to portray Wall Street's political and economic agenda as the result of a democratic process. When it denounced critics of business practices as detestable elitists, it did so because criticism can potentially be very costly. And when it got all worked up about "state power," just like the cult studs do, it did so not out of some delicate Althusserian fear of the ideological apparatus, but for the far simpler and more immediate reason that, if the state were allowed to exercise power as it has in the past, the corporate world might find its taxes raised, its workers all uppity, and its ability to pollute severely constrained.

One of the foundational texts in the market populist tradition was a 1992 book called *The Twilight of Sovereignty* by Walter Wriston, the former CEO of Citibank. Both Wriston personally and Citibank as a whole had bridled for years under the burden of the banking regulations passed in the 1930s. The book's prediction of the demise of state power ("sovereignty") in a coming "information revolution" was very much defined by Wriston's struggle to circumvent these intolerable laws. With government diminished in the coming golden age, we were to have freedom—free markets, that is. Wriston didn't describe this change as a victory for Citibank or for big business; on the contrary, the triumph of markets was to be a triumph for the powerless, who would finally be able to make their will known to the high and the mighty. "Markets are voting machines; they function by taking referenda," Wriston wrote. Markets are "global plebiscites" that pass democratic judgment day and night. Markets are giving "Power to the People."

When empowered by markets and information, the people would naturally use the tools of mass culture to destroy hierarchy. In an ideological homily that would soon become so orthodox that it would color much of the foreign affairs reporting to appear in the U.S., Wriston told how the VCR brought down Marcos, how the cassette tape brought down the Shah, and how TV destroyed communism. So wondrous were these devices' democratic properties, in fact, that when people watch TV they are actually "voting" for the *laissez-faire* way, "for Madonna and Benetton, Pepsi and Prince—but also for democracy, free expression, free markets, and free movement of people and money." Culture warriors might huff about Madonna's bad values, but Wriston, like the cult studs, knew better: To watch the "material girl" prance was to do nothing less than endorse the steel industry's efforts (much lauded in the book) to escape regulation and unionization, to authorize Wriston's own legendary attacks on banking regulation. Consuming was literally revolution.

In the gathering Internet religion of the mid-1990s, Wriston was regarded as a prophet, quoted and name-checked in that "radical" computer industry magazine *Wired* whenever lists of the great thinkers

were called for. *Wired*'s own market populist vision
was even more grandiose than his, however. In the
mid-1990s it hired veteran reporter Jon Katz to
write a column called "The Netizen" in which the
progress of the information revolution would be
theorized and narrated. Katz may not have had a
Ph.D., but he certainly had the same enemies as the
cult studs: In 1997 he authored a culture-warring
tirade called *Virtuous Reality: How America
Surrendered Discussion of Moral Values to Opportunists,
Nitwits, and Blockheads Like William Bennett*. His
"Netizen" columns lashed out at a different elite,
namely the staffers of the "old media" wherever
they might still force their ideas of what's best on
others. For Katz, as for the cult studs, "elitism" was
a matter not of ownership but a certain attitude
towards the people and towards popular intelligence: he established the "elitism" of the hated
"pundits," for example, with the assertion that "they
accused you of being civically dumb, apathetic, and
ignorant." But with the Internet—this "new, democratic, many-to-many model of communication"—all
such top-down discourse would have to end. So
effervescently populist was this new medium that
almost anything associated with it was *ipso facto* an
embodiment of democracy.

Katz's greatest moment came in December 1997, when he announced from the pages of *Wired* that the Internet had now given birth to a powerful new bloc of "digital citizens" who would soon dominate the politics of the nation. Acting in concert with stockbroker Merrill Lynch, *Wired* had commissioned the famous conservative pollster Frank Luntz to do a study of the attitudes of technology users, and Katz had been tapped to reveal the good news to the public. This is what the interactive, back-talking future was to look like: the hyper-democratic "digital citizens" were found to "worship free markets" and to believe that companies were more important than government. Katz took this data and ran with it. The "digital citizen's" love for markets arose from a deep hostility to "rigidly formalized authority." In fact, these market-worshipping Internet users were "startlingly close to the Jeffersonian ideal." Naturally, those who opposed the pro-corporate beliefs of this hot new demographic were dismissed as "political and intellectual elites," tired relics of the old system who "remind [Katz] of the hoary old men in the Kremlin...during the dying days of communism...." This new constituency for the free market was having none of the nostalgia of the older variety. It didn't care about the lost 1950s. It didn't care about family values. All it wanted was the government off its back—and off the backs of the bankers, the manufacturers, and the brokers, while they were at it.

Market populism achieved its most powerful expression in the literature of the booming stock market. Here it was grounded not so much in visions of an "information revolution" but in the fact that a greater percentage of the general public was then investing in stocks than at any time since records were kept. Even though this investment was largely indirect—through mutual funds and 401(k)s—the mere fact of it struck Wall Street as a harbinger of an economic revolution. Maybe Wall Street's long war with Main Street was finally over, the investment banking industry thought; maybe the stock market could recover the position it had lost in the 1930s as the proper guarantor of social welfare. The Street's big thinkers and brokerages rushed to hail the change in the most florid language and imagery they could muster, always returning to the same theme: the power and mighty agency of the common person. Through stock ownership, the once-powerless individual was talking back, was having his or her revenge on the contemptuous elites, was overturning hierarchy and smashing the power structure, was building a kind of economic democracy that "state power" could never hope to achieve. The resulting fantasy of rebellion-through-investing was almost a mirror image of the cult studs' fantasies of rebellion-through-fandom, only slightly more practical, since shareholders actually get to vote on corporate policy.

Peter Lynch, one of the bull market's great ideological figureheads, traced the market populist template in a series of best-selling investment advice books. "Stop listening to professionals!" he insisted, in a blazing anti-elitist manifesto from 1989 called *One Up On Wall Street*. "Any normal person using the customary three percent of the brain can pick stocks just as well, if not better, than the average Wall Street expert." Instead of a complex system for investing Lynch proposed the "power of common knowledge," in which it is one's lowliness that determines one's success in the market. In a move that cult studs would have to envy, Lynch suggested that precisely by absorbing all that sneered-at mass culture we could become great investors and turn the tables on those disdainful elitists. As described in his books, *buy what you know*, the famous Lynchian stock-picking adage, seemed simply to mean, *buy shares in brand names*. And the key to identifying the brands in which to invest was being an alert consumer, a particularly devoted fan. Lynch told of folks who picked stock market "ten-baggers" by contemplating products or brands in the grocery store, at the shopping center, in the food court, at work, and literally in the back yard.

It was the prominent financial journalist Joseph Nocera who transformed Lynch's market populist investment advice into an historical framework for understanding the bull market itself. In his 1994 book, *A Piece of the Action: How the Middle Class Joined the Money Class*, Nocera interpreted each of the consumer financial instruments to appear in the previous thirty years—credit cards, money market accounts, mutual funds—as empowering tools for the common people, each one another step towards "financial democracy," also known as a better percentage. At the end of that long road, naturally, lay the bull market of the 1990s, which differed from all other booms in that it was enriching the good, sweet, average, regular people rather than the bloated aristocrats of Wall Street.

Here, as in so many cult-stud texts, the repugnance of elitism was made to do some pretty heavy lifting. Old-line bankers, for example, are said to have denied the people their rightful percentage out of "snobbery" or "arrogance." The New York Stock Exchange of twenty years ago was described as a "snobbish" "cartel" that answered its critics with "arrogant conceit." Even those figures of financial authority who seek to regulate bankers and stock exchanges—journalists, congressmen, etc.—were said to be motivated by snobbish, arrogant doubts about the intelligence of the people, to seek to protect us from ourselves. But since the bull market of the 1990s was a fairly direct expression of the needs and desires of the middle class, according to Nocera, the way one interpreted its prospects served as a handy indicator of one's commitment to democracy itself: one could either take one's place amongst the bearish elitists and "worry that the 'unsophisticated' small investor would panic at the first sign of trouble and bring the whole thing tumbling down," or "one could applaud it, seeing it as a democratic trend in a democratic society...." Not only were elitists bad people, but their snobbishness had thus caused them to miss out altogether on the wondrous profit-taking of recent years. In fact, the bull market of the '90s was such a grassroots affair, Nocera insisted, that the establishment newspapers didn't even *notice* it until "Main Street" had run the Dow up for two whole years.

One of Wall Street's favorite devices for dramatizing this revolution-through-stockholding was a staged confrontation in which society's weakest members somehow humiliated the suit-wearing authority figures of the old economy. The world was turned gloriously upside down as small-town grandmas from central Illinois beat out the snooty MBAs of Manhattan; as the *soi-disant* "Motley Fools" of the famous personal-finance Website whipped the "wise" investment pros; as the street-wise traders from gritty backgrounds wiped the floor with the effete WASP insiders. "What we have here is nothing short of a revolution," proclaimed Andy Serwer of *Fortune* in the giddy year 1999. "Power that for generations lay with a few thousand white males on a small island in New York City is now being seized by Everyman and Everywoman."

Late-'90s TV commercials for the Discover online brokerage invited us to laugh as a cast of rude, dismissive, old-school executives, yawning and scowling, got well-deserved payback at the hands of an array of humble commoners: tow-truck drivers, hippies, grandmas, and bartenders, all of them down-home Midases who (thanks to the Discover brokerage) owned their own countries, sailed yachts, hobnobbed with royalty, and performed corporate buyouts. TV commercials for the Datek online brokerage showed the common people smashing their way into the stock exchange, breaking down its pretentious doors, pouring through its marble corridors, smashing the glass in the visitors' gallery windows and sending a rain of shards down on the money changers in the pit—all to an insurgent worldbeat tune. It may have looked like the IWW was back, but what the people were overthrowing was merely the senseless "wall" that the voice-over claimed always "stood between you and serious trading." TV commercials for the Charles Schwab online brokerage gave us a cast of real, regular people who had used the brokerage to make real, regular money. "It's the final step in demystification," Charlie Schwab himself told us. "This internet stuff is about freedom. You're in control."

As it turned out, "empowerment" was quite an exercise in mystification itself. With "state power" supine and with the great theorists insisting that this was a time of true financial democracy, small investors got played like a piano. There may yet be cult studs in the land who argue (along with the op-ed page of the *Wall Street Journal*) that even to *believe* in the possibility of manipulation-through-masscult is an elitist error, but as the Nasdaq plunged nearly 70 percent in the first two years of the new century, such high-minded ideas started to seem like just another fantasy of the New Economy bubble. In 2001 and 2002 it was revealed that certain of the great stock-picking personalities of the '90s had in fact exerted considerable influence on prices simply through the power of celebrity pronouncements on CNBC. Other executives had been puffing numbers and cooking books—and deceiving small investors along the way—in order to maximize their options-heavy compensation packages. And the Enron energy conglomerate, a believer in freedom-through-markets so committed that it actually ran commercials comparing itself to the civil rights movement, fessed up to gaming newly deregulated energy markets and essentially to robbing the citizens of California of billions of dollars.

What Business Culture?

Unfortunately, it's difficult to discover what the cult studs themselves made of the parallel world of market populism. For all its generalized hostility to what it called "late capital," cultural studies failed until very late in the decade to produce close analyses of the thought and daily life of business. Convinced that the really important moment of production was not in the factory or the TV studio but in living rooms and on dance floors as audiences made their own meanings from the text of the world around them, the cult studs generally left questions of industry alone. Not only did they fail to notice the anti-elitist and anti-hierarchical talk that was pouring forth from boardrooms, but they weren't interested in noticing it as a matter of principle. I myself found this out in one of my very first brushes with the discipline, when I was working on a Ph.D. about the advertising of the 1960s. In the American Studies workshop I attended I found that, while many of my fellow grad students were studying mass-produced culture, I was just about the only one who was reading industry trade journals or inter-viewing industry leaders. The others regarded this research strategy as being wildly and obviously wrong-headed: clearly I was producing a crude, "top-down" work that would not give due consider-ation to audience reception, at the time virtually the only cultural category to which top-flight graduate students were willing to grant significance. To study what admen thought was tacitly to believe that admen manipulated the public, that audiences were cultural dopes. And what kind of snob believed that? (On the other hand, my peers had a weird tendency to refer to Vance Packard and other mainstream journalistic critics of advertising as adherents of the Frankfurt School, which I think is telling in retro-spect.)

Jim McGuigan attributes this careful avoidance of business issues to "a terror of economic reductionism," a fear that any discussion of matters economic will automatically lead one back to the Marxist determinism of the '30s or—even worse—to the "elitism" of the hated Frankfurt School. One wants to avoid such errors, of course, but why, wonders historian Eric Guthey, have "so many highly trained, intelligent and critical cultural scholars...chosen to overlook so completely the burgeoning corporatization of American culture?" At a time when corporations boast of being related to God and when Microsoft reminds millions of people every day of the meaning of domination, he asks, "isn't this a bit like oceanographers refusing to acknowledge the existence of water?"

Others aren't so generous. Maybe cultural studies' baffling silence on such a critical matter is not so much denial as simple acceptance of market ideology. "Perhaps the stupidity—and there is no better word for it—of some cultural studies is best shown by its stance toward the market," writes communications historian Robert McChesney:

> I have heard leading figures in cultural studies argue
> that the market is not the top-down authoritarian

mechanism that political economists claim, where bosses force the masses to swallow whatever they are fed. To the contrary, they exult, the market is where the masses can contest with the bosses over economic matters; it is a fight without a predetermined outcome. One cultural studies scholar goes so far as to characterize the market as "an expansive popular system."

Cult studs may style themselves radicals, McChesney argues, but many of them have no problems with the free market, with what it gives consumers, with what it does to people's lives. Stephen Adam Schwartz, a scholar of French literature, goes even further than this in an incisive reading of the leaden 1992 anthology. Judging cultural studies' politics by its arguments rather than its chest-thumping vanguardism, Schwartz finds it "strikingly but not surprisingly content-poor, reducing in general to praise for transgression and well-meaning bromides about respect for 'difference.'" Unwilling to distinguish between Western democracies and more rigidly ordered societies, and concerned quite exclusively with self-expression as "the rightful beginning and absolute end of all social and political life," cultural studies turns out to be a close relative of traditional American libertarianism.

This was driven home for me during a radio discussion I participated in a while ago. The BBC had decided that a good way to get me to talk about one of my books was to pair me via satellite with a prominent management theorist and a prominent cult stud. All went well until the conversation slipped into the subject of "personal branding," one of the far-fetched corporate ideas that I had mocked in the book. (Tom Peters has written that we should think of ourselves as brands; I wrote that this was really dehumanizing; you can imagine the rest.) I wasn't surprised to hear the big-name guru stick up for the idea, but I was quite startled to hear the cult stud chime in on his side of the argument, defending personal branding as—what else?—a valuable technique for subversion and individualism. I have been critical of cultural studies for a long time, but I can still remember my dumbstruck astonishment—sitting there with a can of Pepsi in Chicago and listening to these confident voices of Cool Britannia—at this resounding confirmation of all my darkest suspicions.

But one hardly needs a personal experience of this kind to see that the political content of the populist reflex is not what the cult studs believe it to be. There is in fact a new generation of conservative scholars who quite openly make the connection

between cult-stud-style populism and the most rabid
sort of free-market orthodoxy. Perhaps the rise of this
group of thinkers has taken the original, leftist cult
studs by surprise. But it turns out to be a surprisingly
short walk from the active-audience theorizing of the
original to the sterner stuff of market populism.
While the cult studs may have insisted proudly on the
inherent radicalism of their ideas concerning agency,
resistance, and the horror of elitism, as these notions
have been diffused outside the academy their polari-
ties have been reversed; they come across not as
daringly counter-hegemonic but as the most egre-
gious sort of apologia for existing economic arrange-
ments.

Consider, for example, the extremely negative
connotations of the verb "regulate" as it is used in
the cultural studies corpus: almost without variation
it refers to the deplorable actions of an elite even
more noxious than the Frankfurt School, a cabal of
religious conservatives desperately seeking to
suppress difference. And then consider the strikingly
similar negative connotations of the word as it is
used by the *Wall Street Journal*, where it also refers
to the deplorable actions of an obnoxious elite, in
this case meddling liberals who assume arrogantly
that they know better than the market. Both arise

from a form of populism that celebrates critical audiences but that has zero tolerance for critics themselves.

Certain academics are capable of bringing the populism of cultural studies and the populism of the market together with breathtaking ease. Economist Tyler Cowen, for example, translates the populist reflex into an extended celebration of the benevolence of markets, wandering here and there over the entire history of art in his 1998 book, *In Praise of Commercial Culture*, seeking always to prove that the market deserves the credit for all worthwhile cultural production. The market guarantees quality. The market guarantees diversity. And have you ever considered who pays the bills for all those artists? That's right: the market. As it turns out, the market maintains the strong record it does (over the centuries, according to Cowen's accounting, batting real close to 1.000) because it is indistinguishable from the people. And "an audience," he writes, "is more intelligent than the individuals who create their entertainment." Those who recognize popular intelligence are "cultural optimists," in whose camp Cowen puts himself, Gans, and a handful of leading cult studs, all of whom wisely believe in letting the people and the market make their decisions without interference. On the other side, meanwhile, stands a motley group of critics united only by their shared "elitism," the conviction that they know best. From the Frankfurt School (who come in for severe chastisement) to the Christian right, they are all "cultural pessimists," doubtful about the people's capacity to decide for themselves, skeptical about popular tastes, contemptuous of progress itself. As even the Nazis can be made to fit under such a broad definition of "pessimism," Cowen brings them in, too.

Advertising scholar James Twitchell crosses the bridge from cultural studies to market populism with more diplomacy and style. In his 1999 celebration of consumerism, *Lead Us Into Temptation*, the debate is again about popular intelligence. Do intellectuals think the public is stupid or smart? Powerless and impotent or bursting with agency? Clearly, according to Twitchell, most culture critics fall into the former camp, seeing "the consumer as a dumb ox." Appearing in their usual role as the worst snobs ever are the Frankfurt School, who dared to criticize the makers of mass culture on the grounds that they sometimes tricked consumers, and that they, the arrogant professors, somehow knew better. Twitchell rejects such an argument—and also rejects Ralph Nader, Vance Packard, John Kenneth Galbraith, and presumably anyone else who has ever criticized corporate America—not because he wants to see corporate profits grow without the interference of the regulations that those men's work inspired, but because he loves democracy, he loves We the People. The fact is, he reminds us, audiences are active, not passive. "Watching television," he writes, "is almost frantic with creative activity." Consumers are *never* "duped," a point Twitchell makes three times in five pages; consumers are, in actuality, "the ones with the power, continually negotiating new sites for meaning." Twitchell does not write, "consumers will be the ones with the power once certain regulations are in place"; they have the power *now*, as they have had it always, through the medium of the free market. So great are our wisdom and our agency that we don't just create some subcultural response to mass culture; *we create the mass culture itself!* By watching, by buying, we authorize all:

> I never want to imply that, in creating order in our lives, consumption *is* doing something to us that we are not covertly responsible for. We are not victims of consumption. Just as we make our media, our media make us. Again, commercialism is *not* making us behave against our "better judgment." Commercialism *is* our better judgment.

Strictly speaking, we may not have voted for the New Economy, with all its grotesque inequality and its smashing of the local, but we have authorized its every act anyway, just by consuming. Turning to the globalization and cyber-economy of the late '90s, Twitchell writes in his conclusion that, "We have not just asked to go this way, we have demanded." Consumerism is democracy, the veritable "triumph of the popular will." To criticize its workings is to express contempt for the judgment of the people themselves.

Outside the academy the translation of cultural studies into market populism was even more pronounced. Granted, newspaper stories on the cult studs rarely manage to do much more than giggle at the spectacle of people with Ph.D.s writing about Barbie and *The Simpsons*, but the cult studs' trade-mark language of audience agency and subversive subtexts seeped down to earth nonetheless. Journalists who absorbed the populist reflex could be heard calling on readers to rally around the communitarian teachings of the Teletubbies or wondering whether anyone had the right to dislike the Spice Girls. Recently Edward Rothstein of the *New York Times* even managed to work a 9/11 angle into the by now familiar story of disdainful snobs vs.

we the audience, depicting none other than Osama bin Laden as the latest recruit to Theodor Adorno's axis of cultural elitism.

The confusion of market populism with broader human liberation comes into high relief when we make a hard right from the popular press to the realm of high libertarian ideology. *Reason* magazine is formally dedicated to "free minds and free markets" but its most remarkable editorial achievement can be found in a curious journalistic stunt that its cast of writers performs over and over again. Our patriotic American belief in the intelligence of the common people, also known as consumers, is made to collide violently with the nose of whoever is besieging this month's corporation-in-distress. Agency, that cult-stud staple, is recast by *Reason* into the silver bullet of corporate defense: here agency means the people express themselves perfectly well through the market, through consumer choice; it means that neither the government nor industry groups have any business protecting anybody from anything; best of all, it transforms those who criticize industry into the worst sort of (you guessed it) snobs and elitists, tacitly believing that the public are a collection of agency-deprived fools.

Like the works of Herbert Gans, *Reason* never comes up in the monographs and anthologies of the cult studs. And yet one wishes that, if only to temper their endless culture-war *gasconade*, the cult studs could somehow be required to take a peek beneath the publication's Easter-egg colored covers. There they will find a militantly pro-corporate right that, like consumer society itself, has no problem with difference, lifestyle, and pleasure; that cares not a whit for the preservation of disciplinary boundaries; that urges the destruction of cultural hierarchy in language as fervid as anything to appear in the pages of *Social Text*. There are even fairly exact parallels to the familiar cultural studies argument. A 1998 *Reason* feature story by anthropologist Grant McCracken, for example, celebrates the "plenitude" of endless lifestyle diversity as "the signature gesture of our culture." After chewing out the usual right-wing culture warriors (Bennett, Buchanan, Robertson) and dropping the obligatory bomb on the Frankfurt School (Herbert Marcuse was also singled out for article-length punishment in the magazine's November 1998 issue), McCracken hails the rise of "difference, variety, and novelty" and advises his comrades to forget about suppressing the Other and to adjust themselves instead to the "inevitable." Declaring a democratic interest in even

the oddest cultural novelties, McCracken informs
his conservative colleagues that

> Line dancing provides an interesting and dynamic
> site for the transformation of gender, class, outlook,
> and, yes, politics. It is on the dance floor that cultural
> categories and social rules are being re-examined and,
> sometimes, reinvented.

Of course, the only thing that can make sense out of
this world of endless differentiation is "the great
lingua franca" of "the marketplace." It is capitalism
that's breaking "the stranglehold of hierarchies and
elites"; it is the "consumer culture" that "is a cause
and a consequence of plenitude."

Other *Reason*ers cite the great cult studs explicitly
when making their trademark argument. Editor Nick
Gillespie grounds his 1996 defense of the movie
industry in the populist reflex as an established principle of legitimate social science, citing prominent
cult stud Constance Penley (best known for her work
on pornographic fanzines in which the *Star Trek*
characters get it on) as the authority for this most
hallowed of culturisms: "All viewers or consumers
have 'agency': they *process* what they see or hear—
they do not merely lap it up." Before long Gillespie

moves on to the inevitable flip side: the elitism of the entertainment industry's critics. These are figures who believed that "viewers lack virtually any critical faculties or knowledge independent of what program producers feed them," that "the idiot box...turns viewers into idiots," that we consumers are "robotic stooges," "trained dogs," "dumb receivers," "unwitting dupes." Not that they say any of this about us in public, mind you. These are simply *implied*, the obvious consequence of their "top-down conception of culture," their focus on "authorial intentions," and the equally obvious and far more loathsome corollary, that "they know best," that "the viewer simply can't be trusted," that "regulation by the government" was in order.

Ah, but the market, the glorious, diversity-driven market, makes no such elitist presumptions. Not only does the market permit all the excellent examples of "resisting readers" that Gillespie finds so dope (the scoffing robots of *Mystery Science Theater 3000*, for example), but in the land of pop culture, "as with all market-based exchanges, knowledge, value, and power...are dispersed." The robots mock a lousy movie, ergo the government must leave Microsoft alone. QED.

The libertarian version of the populist reflex can be quite versatile. After looking through back issues of *Reason* I found it deployed on behalf of the advertising industry (we aren't fooled 100 percent of the time, you know), the tobacco industry (people choose to smoke cigarettes, you know), the gun industry (not all kids murder their classmates, you know), Barnes & Noble (people choose to go there, you know), Microsoft (choice incarnate, you know), Jesse Ventura, whose election as governor of Minnesota gave our Mr. Gillespie an opportunity to explain his populism in historical detail (complete with passages about the affection that is felt by the good people of Minnesota toward corporations), and this towering whopper, which came up as an explanation of, well, just about everything: "at the end of the twentieth century, 'money power'—indeed, power in general—is far more concentrated in government hands than in corporate ones."

Believe it or not, the same logic can also be found in everyday use even further to the right. While the luminous names of the great cult studs may be entirely unfamiliar to the fulminating Rush Limbaugh, their trademark arguments concerning democracy through pop culture and the essential elitism of those who criticize it are as friendly and familiar to him as the winning smile of Ollie North. Rush's version of the populist reflex comes across with particular vigor in his 1993 collection of witticisms, *See, I Told You So*, in which he refers to his own rise as an object lesson in the fundamental justice of markets, as in this rousing invocation of decentered power and audience agency: "Nobody put me in that [dominant] position—no network, no government program, no producer. You in the audience who have voluntarily tuned the dial to my voice—you alone—have caused my success." On the other side of the coin from the "magic of the marketplace," of course, are the high-handed, top-down, know-it-all regulators who want "to use this country as their grand laboratory experiment." But meddling liberals are just the tip of the hegemony iceberg: even worse is the "sheer arrogance" of the elitists who believe that "people who listen to my show are just too stupid to tackle America's complicated problems." After all this, the reader is only marginally surprised when Rush proceeds to wheel out the Frankfurt School, this time in the person of Theodor Adorno, for its ritual thumping.

Making History Just As They Please

For all the talk of cultural disintegration from one side, and of intolerance and persecution from the other, it is surprising how much basic agreement there was beneath the stormy surface of the culture wars. However Americans might squabble over funding for the NEA, educated people everywhere could agree on one thing: the perfidy of cultural elitism. And whether they simply ignored the world of business or actively extolled the corporate order, both sides agreed that our newfound faith in active, intelligent audiences made criticism of the market philosophically untenable. Taste was annexed to politics in the 1990s in a manner that trivialized both, redefining democracy as a matter of demographic representation, as a posture of exaggerated humility before the wisdom of the people. One caught glimpses of the new consensus in movies like *Pleasantville*, where smugness about the liberated present arose phoenix-like from the ashes of the old, gray flannel smugness. It may have been a consensus of masturbating moms rather than muffin-baking moms; of dreadlocked millionaires rather than horn-rimmed millionaires; of Kirk and Spock fisting rather than exploring new galaxies; of culture war rather than cold war; but it was as confident about the glories of life in these United States as any intellectual order has ever been.

If cultural studies has a unique intellectual virtue, it is a willingness to acknowledge its own failings, and in this essay I have made liberal use of the work of several of the discipline's most prominent critics. But in many other ways cultural studies looks, reads, behaves, and legitimates just like its never-acknowledged consensus ancestor. For all the cult studs' populist pretensions, the dominant tone of much of their writing is one of bombastic self-congratulation and vainglorious blaring—sometimes self-pitying, sometimes pompous beyond belief. Even more indicative of the hardening of a new consensus is the cult studs' strange fantasy of encirclement by Marxists at once crude and snobbish, a transplanted Cold War chimera that one found repeated in just about every one of the discipline's texts, that filled the e-mail signature lines of the academically stylish.*

The point here isn't merely that the right and the cult studs use the same target for bayonet practice, but simply that their target is a straw man, that they ignore the facts of cultural life out of a misplaced anxiety over a cartoonish doctrine they imagine as both Teutonic and red, a horrifying cross between the nation's historical enemies. "Each generation is driven to theorize by the particular historical tendencies and events that confront it," Lawrence Grossberg and Cary Nelson wrote way back in 1988. And yet while the cult studs fought the

---

*I am referring here to a thirty-year-old proclamation by Situationist Raoul Vaneigem that seemed to turn up everywhere in 1997 and 1998. "People who talk about revolution and class struggle without referring explicitly to everyday life, without understanding what is subversive about love and what is positive in the refusal of constraint, have corpses in their mouths." This may have made sense in Paris '68, but its enthusiastic repeating across the cultural studies left of the late 1990s betokens a misguided conviction that—at the very peak of the New Economy, the moment of the corporate world's greatest triumph—the people who really needed defying in America were those who "talk about revolution and class struggle."

obvious fight with the Christian right, they seemed almost completely to miss the history of their own era. Business publications were crowing that the production and export of culture was becoming the central element of the American economy; they saw the millennium in the conquest of the world by Monsanto and Microsoft. But up on the heights from which critical fire could have been brought to bear on their imperial parade, the self-proclaimed radicals were busy tying themselves in knots to avoid any taint of vulgar Marxism.

That is, I think, an optimistic take. What seems far more likely is that, as the most committed of the original cult studs drift away and turn their attention to more relevant subjects (sweatshops, the crisis in academic labor, etc.), cultural studies as a discipline will evolve to a point where matters economic are simply defined away, where any transgression is as meaningful as any other, and where the next crop of cult studs can take the logical step from academy to consultancy work for the growing number of hip ad agencies and ethnographic-based market research firms, celebrating the subversive potential of Sprite or the Escalade without reservation or troubling doubt.

Consider in this regard the cult studs' marked complacency about their own role in the larger cultural economy. To be sure, the duties and responsibilities of intellectuals is a subject with which they are deeply, obsessively concerned: Andrew Ross, for example, brilliantly dissects the power of intellectuals to "designate what is legitimate" in *No Respect*. But in Ross' telling the cult studs themselves appear only as a solution to the shameful history of academic snobbery and collaboration with the bad guys. Ross does not consider what might happen when the bad guys decided they didn't care anymore about the old high-culture markers of legitimacy and wanted instead to prattle on about subversive ad campaigns and tattooed entrepreneurs and the heroism of the change agent. After leading readers through a century of snobs and aristocratic Trotskyites, Ross concludes his story of intellectuals and popular culture by locating himself and his colleagues (the non-elitist "new intellectuals") on the high plateau of historical accomplishment where such behavior by academics is simply no longer possible. This was a hopeful prediction but just as wrong as Herbert Gans' prediction in 1974. What we got instead was a fatal double irony: academic radicalism became functionally indistinguishable from free market theory at exactly the historical moment when capitalist managers decided it was time to start referring to themselves as "radicals," to understand consumption itself as democracy.

These days, in advertising agencies and market-research firms worldwide, the gap between critical intellectuals and simple salesmanship seems only to shrink. With or without the assistance of the cult studs, American audiences are growing more skeptical by the minute; fashion cycles that once required years now take months; heroes of the age are despised by the people in spite of the best efforts of *Fortune* and *Time*. The intellectual task at hand is not just legitimation, it is infiltration, and suddenly questions like the subversive potential of *That '70s Show* aren't quite as academic as they once seemed. Yes, career-minded students are still interested in deep understandings of fan communities and audience "resistance," but not so much to celebrate these things as learn how to work with them or around them, so that they can someday go on to produce commercials that flatter a subculture's paranoia or that use the more standard techniques of prude-dissing or let-you-be-you-ing to get, as the admen put it, "under the radar." The active-audience creed of the cult stud has thus become less an article of radical faith and more a practical foundation for aspiring copywriters or marketing experts, who can be found commenting in highbrow business publications on the need to "reenchant" the brand with a "liberatory postmodernism." One day they're attentively following the *X-Files* listserv or studying the counter-hegemonic funeral wailing of the Warao people; the next they're inventing brands for a nation of alienated 7-Eleven shoppers and hege-mony-smashing mallwalkers. Maybe the corporate university and the academic left have something in common after all. ■